OLD
Plantation Hymns

AMS PRESS
NEW YORK

OLD

Plantation Hymns

A collection of hitherto unpublished melodies of the
slave and the freedman, with historical
and descriptive notes.

BY

WILLIAM E. BARTON, D.D.

Author of "A Hero in Homespun."

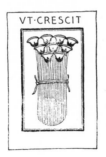

Lamson, Wolffe and Company

Boston   New York   London

MDCCCXCIX

Library of Congress Cataloging in Publication Data

Barton, William Eleazar, 1861-1930.
  Old plantation hymns.

  Original t.p. reads: Old plantation hymns; a
collection of hitherto unpublished melodies of the
slave and the freeman, with historical and descriptive
notes.
  Reprint of the 1899 ed.
  1. Negro songs. I. Title.
ML3556.B29 1972   784.7'56   72-38499
ISBN 0-404-09918-1

Reprinted from an original copy in the collections
of the Union Theological Seminary of New York

From the edition of 1899, Boston and New York
First AMS edition published in 1972
Manufactured in the United States of America

AMS PRESS INC.
NEW YORK, N. Y.   10003

OLD PLANTATION HYMNS.

By William E. Barton, D. D.

ONE of the most genuine surprises ever given to lovers of music occured in 1871, when a company of students from Fisk University started North, to earn money for that school by singing the plantation hymns of their parents. When Henry Ward Beecher admitted them to Plymouth Church, the papers had not a little to say in a joking way of "Beecher's Negro Minstrels." To the surprise of everybody, the moderate success for which the promoters of the scheme had hoped and the dismal failure which the beginnings of the enterprise prophesied were both forgotten in a most brilliant campaign upon both sides of the ocean, resulting in the building of Jubilee Hall and in the publication of the "Jubilee Songs," by voice and press, wherever the English language is known and even beyond. The story of these negro boys and girls singing their quaint, weird songs before crowned heads reads like a romance. The continued popularity of the airs then first introduced is attested by their use at all manner of occasions, from funerals to yachting parties, and their republication in all manner of books, from collections of Sunday-school melodies to books of college songs. Whatever the critic may say about them,—and what he says is usually divided between praise and astonishment,—there is no denying their power. Many of us have seen great congregations swayed by them as a field of grain before the wind. Dvorak calls their tunes our only characteristic American music, and his suite based on their airs is well known. To critics and to common people they are alike enjoyable.

There is a good deal of danger that we shall not discover many of these songs not already familiar. The growing conditions among the negroes are unfavorable to the making of new songs, and the ground has been pretty well hunted over for the old ones. It would be a thing quite worth while to discover a new or old one as sweet as "Swing low, sweet chariot," or as quaint as "Turn back Pharaoh's army," or as pathetic and powerful as "Steal away." If anyone knows any such, he ought to see that they are preserved, both words and music.

It was the writer's privilege to live in the South from 1880 till 1887, and to come into contact with a good many kinds of people. During the earlier years especially he made careful records of most that interested him, and he supplemented these records as the years went by with whatever came in his way. One of the things which never was allowed to escape was an odd song, secular or religious; and wherever possible the quaint air as well as the words was written down at the time. These have waited for eleven years, and it is time that they were printed if they are to appear at all. It is possible that some have been printed already; but even if so, the variations will be of interest. The most of them, however, are probably new to almost all who will see them here, and many, I am confident, have never been printed or even written before.

Conspicuous among the religious songs of the colored people, as of the white people in the Cumberland Mountains, is the large group of "Family Songs," in which the chief or only variation in the successive stanzas is the substitution of "father," "mother," or other relative in order. One of the most unique of these is,

3

HOWDY, HOWDY!

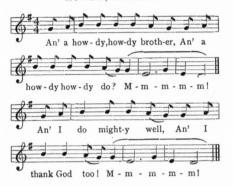

An' a how-dy, how-dy broth-er, An' a
how-dy how-dy do? M-m-m-m-m!
An' I do might-y well, An' I
thank God too! M-m-m-m-m!

DOWN IN THE VALLEY TO PRAY.

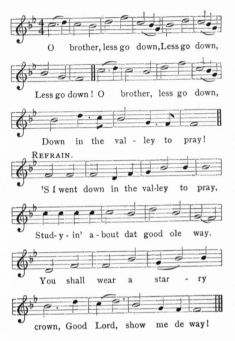

O brother, less go down, Less go down,
Less go down! O brother, less go down,
Down in the val-ley to pray!
REFRAIN.
'S I went down in the val-ley to pray,
Stud-y-in' a-bout dat good ole way.
You shall wear a star-ry
crown, Good Lord, show me de way!

This is the entire hymn, except that it goes on to greet, and be greeted by, the sisters, mothers, fathers, preachers and mourners of the company. It is a song for the opening of service; and no type can indicate its warmth and fervor. The "M-m-m-m-m" is a humming sound with closed lips. Any one who will close the lips and hum this sound will discern something of the perfectly delicious expression of the joy of meeting.

There are several songs that tell of going down in the valley to pray. The valley seems to the colored Christian the proper place for all prayer save that of ecstatic fervor; and that fervor voices itself in song rather than in prayer. Prayer, to the negro, was so commonly associated with the thought of trouble that often had no other outlet, that all the drapery of the valley seemed to fit its mental association. Sometimes he rose to sing,

"When I git up on de mountain top,
I'll shout an' shout and nebber stop."

Or,

"I'll praise de Lord an' nebber stop!"

but this shout or praise was either song or hallelujah—it was not commonly prayer. One of these songs, with a very pretty melody, is given here. The words are similar to those of a song used by the Jubilee singers, but the melody is different.

This song does not usually follow through the family in order, but, being in the nature of an exhortation, addresses the "mourners," "sinners," "seekers," etc. The "mourners" of these songs, it should be remembered, are not necessarily those in affliction, but those who frequent the "mourners' bench" and have not yet "got through." Some of these songs inform these mourners that,

"When I was a mourner just like you,
I prayed and prayed till I got through."

Not "till I got through mourning" or praying, but till that necessary intermediate state, that limbo bordering upon regeneration, was passed. A period of "mourning" is counted a prerequisite for conversion.

The music in this piece is very expressive. The word "down" has always a descending note, and in the first and third lines covers three notes, *re, do, la;* the word "pray" falls as it were to its knees on the dominant below and is held for four beats.

So many of the negro songs are solemn and in 2:2 or 4:4 time, that when one trips along in 2:4 time with a lively step it is worth noticing. One of these, in which the Christian way is neither a struggle nor a climb, but a joyous progress with confident hope, and almost gleeful measure, is

GOIN' OVER ON DE UDDAH SIDE OF JORDAN.

The B flat in the fourth line is meant to suggest a slight variation of tone which cannot be written.

In this, as in many such songs, the melody turns back to the refrain almost before the stanza is completed, so that the held "O!" belongs almost as much to the end of one line as the beginning of the next. The stanzas then take up "my sister," "my mother," and other godly relatives, but "my Lord" is retained in each.

One of the most effective uses of syncopation which I have ever heard is in the song "Tell Bruddah 'Lijah!" or "No harm!" Brother Elijah is probably the prophet, for there is no human character in the Bible too great to be counted a "brother," and some of the allusions to "Brer Jonah" and "Brer Simon Peter" are as unexpected as can well be imagined.

In this hymn the explosive stress upon the word "Sinnah" is startling; and the question, "Ain' you tired of sinnin'?" is wonderfully direct.

TELL BRUDDAH LIJAH.

2—O mourner!
Ain' you tired ob mournin'?
Lay down your load ob hell
An' come along to Jesus!

3—O Christian!
Ain' you tired ob prayin'?
I've laid down my load ob hell
An' come along to Jesus!

4—O preachers!
Ain' you tired ob shoutin'?
I've laid down my load ob hell
An' walk de road wid Jesus!

A corrupted version of a Jubilee song is familiar to many people, called "Sooner in de Morning." It should not be "sooner," but "soon," or early. Another song with the same burden, but very different tune, I have often heard in meetings of colored people. There is a marked contrast between the two parts of its melody, the refrain keeping the middle registers, and the verses swinging much lower, beginning an octave below the first part, about middle C. It is a major melody, and moves almost entirely in thirds. The few intermediate tones are quite as likely to be accidentals as to take other notes of the diatonic scale: indeed, the negro rarely sings the seventh note true, to a musical instrument, but generally flats it more or less as in the minor scales. Fondness for these slightly variable tones suggests a reason for the negro's love of a banjo or violin.

SOON IN DE MORNING.

REFRAIN.

I'm goin' up home soon in de morn - ing,
D.C. *O yon-dah stands de two tall an - gels,*

goin' up home soon in de morn - ing,
yon - dah stands de two tall an - gels,

I'm goin' up home soon in de
O yon - dah stands de two tall

FINE.

morn - ing, I'm goin' to live with God.
an - gels, I'm goin' to live with God.

I dun-no what my brother wants to stay here

for ! Stay here for ! Stay here for ! I

dun - no what my broth - er wants to

D.C.

stay here for ! I'm goin' to live with God !

2—I dunno what the sinner wants to stay here for, etc.

3—I dunno what the preacher wants to stay here for, etc.

4—I dunno what the deacons want to stay here for, etc.

This song is quite in line with the view of the world which most of these hymns present. The world is a wilderness; the Christian has a hard time; and heaven is his home. The thought comes out in "Mighty Rocky Road." It is a melody in 2:4 time, and trips along over the rocks very lightly, rising a full octave at a flight at the thought of being "most done trabbelin'." It is an excellent illustration of the way in which the twin birth of these words and notes fitted them to each other.

MIGHTY ROCKY ROAD.

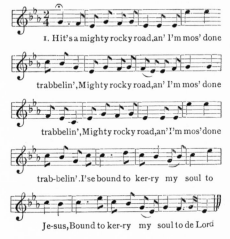

1. Hit's a mighty rocky road, an' I'm mos' done

trabbelin', Mighty rocky road, an' I'm mos' done

trabbelin', Mighty rocky road, an' I'm mos' done

trab-belin'. I'se bound to ker-ry my soul to

Je-sus, Bound to ker-ry my soul to de Lord

2—Christian's on de road, an' he's mos' done trabbelin', etc.

3—Mourner's on de road, an' he's mos' done trabbelin', etc.

4—Sinner's on de road, an' he's a long time trabbelin', etc.

5—Dis a rough, rocky road, an' I'm mos' done trabbelin', etc.

The tune to the last song has a swing not unlike the war-time melody,

"Great big brick house, an' nobody libin' in't,
Nobody libin' in't, nobody libin' in't,
Great big brick house, an' nobody libin' in't,
Down in Alabam,"

to which air are sung words whence a popular college song borrows the lines,

"Hain't I glad to git out de wilderness,
Leaning on de Lamb."

It was in Alabama, by the way, that I got the song, "New Born Again," whose rising and syncopated "Free grace, free grace, free grace, sinner," make the grace more ample with each repetition. It has a certain dignity combined with light joyousness which our Gospel Hymns often strive for in vain. Indeed, there are several things for us to learn from these songs.

NEW BORN AGAIN.

Hal - le - lu - jah! Hal - le - lu - jah!

New-born a - gain. Been a long time

talk-in',Bout a start - in' on de way.

Free grace! Free grace! Free grace, sin - ner!

2—Free grace! free grace! free grace, brother!

3—Free grace! free grace! free grace, sister!

4—Free grace! free grace! free grace, mourner!

Another song represents the journey through life in another way. It is not a two-step nor a gay procession, but a solemn yet confident march. It is in stately 4:4 time, and has the suggestion of a quiet but effective drumbeat on its accented notes.

WALK THROUGH THE VALLEY IN PEACE.

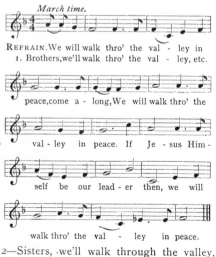

March time.

REFRAIN.We will walk thro' the val - ley in
1. Brothers,we'll walk thro' the val - ley, etc.

peace,come a - long,We will walk thro' the

val - ley in peace. If Je - sus Him -

self be our lead - er then, we will

walk thro' the val - ley in peace.

2—Sisters, we'll walk through the valley, etc.

3—Peter done walked on the water, etc.

4—Daniel done walked through the lions' den, etc.

At a meeting which I used to attend

frequently, one of the leading singers was Sister Bemaugh, who often started the tune. One night there came from another settlement a famous singer, a man, who quite usurped Sister Bemaugh's place. There was no denying that she felt it, as he stood up before the congregation whenever a hymn was called for, in a most comfortable frame of mind, his head turned well to the left and the thumb and finger of his right hand holding the tip of his left ear, as he sang song after song. Many of the songs were new to the congregation, and were sung as solos, and he liked them none the less on that account. Several times Sister Bemaugh attempted to start a song; but each time he was ahead of her. At first she joined in the singing; but at length, discouraged and displeased, she gave it up and sat silent. The meeting held late, and Sister Bemaugh, who usually stayed to the very end, prepared to go. She got her lantern, which she had left in one of the front corners, and was somewhat ostentatiously lighting a match, when a hymn was called for,—and the visiting brother could think of none. It was Sister Bemaugh's opportunity. She quickly lighted and turned down the wick, and began to sing, "My good old Auntie's gone along"; and all the congregation fell in with her. I can see her now, as in the dimly lighted tobacco barn where the meeting was held she stood holding her lantern and singing. She was slender and had high cheek bones, but her face was pleasant, and her voice had a certain soul-quality, with a ring of satisfaction. Almost every other note in the song is chromatic, and it is no small task to sing it well; but Sister Bemaugh sang it to perfection, standing and leading, as a woman does not commonly do, and having sung it to the end, she went along. If the reader will pick out the notes of this song on the piano, and then sing it, swaying slowly, I think he will like it.

GONE ALONG.

1. My good old aun - tie's gone a -

long, She's gone a - long, She's gone a -

long, My good old aun - tie's gone a -

long, Gone across bold Jor - dan's stream.

REFRAIN.

Thank God, she's got re - li-gion, I do be -

lieve, I do be - lieve, I do believe. Thank

God, she's got re - li - gion, I do be -

lieve, Gone a - cross bold Jor-dan's stream.

2—My good old mother's gone along.

3—My good old father's gone along.

4—My good old brother's gone along.

5—My good old sister's gone along.

No classification of negro hymns is entirely satisfactory; but a very large class is made up of a refrain to which is sung a series of verses in variable order, often having no special relation to the refrain. Many of them are used with scores of different songs, and never twice in the same order. Some present a slight variation in the refrain, but have a uniform response. Of these I have a large number. One very rare one, and one that I count among the best, is "Cold Icy Hand." The burden of the song is the response, "Death goner lay his cold icy hand on me." An indescribable effect is given to the "cold icy hand" by a

syncopation. The word "cold" has the accent of the downward beat, and the first syllable of "icy" takes a half note in the middle of the measure. The surprise of the shock which this gives to the nerves, together with the weird tune which prepares one for any uncanny effect, is not unlike the touch of a cold hand. The effect is not less uncanny in the third line of the refrain, in an accidental flat or natural given to the word "cryin'." It is a wail like that of a lost soul.

COLD, ICY HAND.

1. O sin - ner! Sin-ner! you bet-ter pray! Or your soul be lost at de jedg-ment day!

Death goner lay his cold, i - cy hand on me! Death goner lay his cold, i - cy hand on me!

REFRAIN.

Cry - in', O Lord! Cry - in', O my

Lord! Cry-in', O Lord, Death goner lay his

cold, i - cy hand on me.

2—O, sinner, you be careful how you walk on de cross,—
Or your foot may slip an' you' soul be los'.

In all these hymns the notes must adjust themselves to variations in metre. The words of successive stanzas vary in length, and the notes must be varied also. In writing the notes one has to compromise. In singing, they must be adjusted to the different verses, as:

1. O sin - ner! Sin - ner! you bet - ter pray!

2. O sinner, you be careful how you walk on the cross.

The foregoing song uses principally stanzas that have reference to death, and contain a warning; but among a great collection of them there is no certain order. Several hymns in common use furnish couplets for this purpose,—most of all, "Jesus my all to heaven is gone." Other hymns are used. I have the music—strikingly like that of one of our college songs— of one hymn which uses half a stanza of "Am I a soldier of the cross?" and it is quite effective used in this way, with the question of the first half unanswered. It is one of the few negro hymns which requires a bass clef. The body of the hymn is sung in unison—the response being sung in bass and all accordant parts.

In the published Jubilee songs, the harmony has been added for piano and quartette; but it is rarely found in negro songs.

In this particular song, there is no refrain, the lines being repeated several times to make up a stanza out of half of one. Another hymn, which is sung also by the white people of the Cumberland Mountains, takes the hymn "Did Christ o'er sinners weep," and fits to its stanzas a refrain:

"This world is not my home,
This world is not my home;
This world's a howling wilderness,
This world is not my home."

THIS WORLD IS NOT MY HOME.

2—The Son of God in tears
   The wondering angels see.
   Be thou astonished, O my soul,
   He shed those drops for thee.

The melody above is smooth, flowing and restful, and while sad is not hopeless. It sounds well with the words to which it is wedded.

I have one song which starts in with an introduction which has little to do either in words or music with what follows and which belongs only to the opening stanza, or rather to the first use of the refrain. It is not unlike the recitative which precedes a formal movement, and with change of tempo.

SOLDIER OF THE CROSS.

1—Am I a soldier of the cross,
   A follower of the Lamb?

2—Must I be carried to the skies
   On flowery beds of ease?

3—Are there no foes for me to face,
   Must I not stem the flood?

4—Sure I must fight if I would reign,
   Increase my courage, Lord.

HEAVEN BELLS RINGIN' IN MY SOUL.

RECITATIVE.

No-bod-y knows who I am, . .

who I be till de com-in' day.

REFRAIN. (*Twice as fast.*)

O de heav'n bells ring-in'! De sing-sol-

singin'! Heav'n bells a-ringin' in my soul!

Gwine a-way to see my Je-sus,

Gwine a-way to see my Lord.

O de heav'n bells ring-in'! De sing-sol

singin'! Heav'n bells a-ring-in' in my soul!

1. { Walked a-round from door to door,
      What to do I did not know

Heav'n bells a-ring'-in' in my soul!
Heav'n bells a-ring'-in' in my soul!

2—I'm a-comin' to de Lord, I'm a-comin'
    up too,
    Heaven bells ringin' in my soul;
    I'm comin' to de Lord till heaven I
    view,
    Heaven bells ringin' in my soul.

3—Heaven is a high an' a lofty place,
    Heaven bells ringin' in my soul;
    But you can't git dar ef you hain't got
    grace,
    Heaven bells ringin' in my soul.

Some of these refrains are little
more than reiterated ejaculations, the
monotony of which is somewhat re-
lieved by the variable character of the
couplets which make up the stanzas.

SWEET HEAVEN.

REFRAIN.

Oh, sweet heav-en! Oh, sweet heav-en!

FINE.

O sweet heav-en! But how I long to be there.

1. { Some people think that I have no grace. But
     I'll see my Sav-iour face to face; Lord,

D.C.

how I long to be there.
how I long to be there.

2—I have a right to the tree of life,
    And how I long to be there!
    With them that fought my Jesus' fight,
    And how I long to be there!

3—The grace of God do reign so sweet,
    And how I long to be there!
    It spread abroad, both home and
    abroad,
    Lord, how I long to be there!

4—The tallest tree in Paradise,
    Lord, how I long to be there!
    The Christian calls it the tree of life,
    O, how I long to be there!

5—If you get there before I do,
    O, how I long to be there!
    Look out for me, I'm coming too,
    O, how I long to be there!

In much of our modern preaching
the emphasis has shifted from the life
to come to that which now is; and
sometimes good advice about diet and
hygiene, and of righteousness as tend-
ing to longevity hold the place once
given to immortality. It is not so in
plantation theology. The thought of
heaven is constantly to the fore.

The resurrection is a favorite theme
in these songs, and its figures are well
supplied by Ezekiel's vision. Among
them is one that is very simple in its
movement, starting with plain quarter
notes in 4:4 movement, but growing
irregular in the refrain, and using
with effect a syncopation on, "An' a
Lawd," and bringing in a strong up-
ward swing on the long first syllable
of "mawnin'."

DESE DRY BONES OF MINE.

1. What kind of shoes is dem you wear?
Dat you may walk up - on de air,

Come to - ged - der in de mawn - in'.
Come to - ged - der in de mawn - in'.

REFRAIN.

An' a Lawd, dese dry bones of mine . .

Shall come to-ged-der in de mawn - in'.

2—If you get dah befo' I do,
Come togeddah in de mawnin'!
Look out for me, I'm comin' too,
Come togeddah in de mawnin'!

The ease with which this rising is to be accomplished in the world to come, has its contrast in a song of rising in the present life. Here Satan appears, and is a familiar figure in negro songs. It is to be noted that while he is a very real and terrible personage, there is always a lively, almost mirthful suggestion in the mention of his name. The melody of this song could not be wedded to a very serious line of thought. The singers appear to feel little troubled over Satan's easy advantage, but cheerfully throw upon him the responsibility for the difficulty of their earthly rising.

The personality of Satan is, therefore, at once a terror and a source of enjoyment to the negro. The place he holds in negro theology is not unlike that which he occupied in the miracle plays of the middle ages.

There seems an inherent tendency to insincerity in negro demonology. Satan is a decided convenience. It is always possible to load upon him what else must be a weight upon the conscience. That Satan holds the sinner responsible for this has its compensation again in the fact that Satan himself is to be dethroned.

HARD TO RISE AGAIN.

REFRAIN.

O Sa - tan comes like a bu-sy ole man,

Hal - ly, O hal - ly, O hal - le - lu!

He gets you down at de foot-y of de hill,

Hal - ly, O hal - ly, O hal - le - lu!

He gets you down at de foot-y of de hill,

FINE.

Hard to rise a - gain.

1. { Je - sus, my all to heaven is gone,
He whom I fix my hopes up - on,

Hal - ly, O hal - ly, O hal - le - lu! }
Hal - ly, O hal - ly, O hal - le - lu! }

He whom I fix my hopes up - on,

D.C.

Hard to rise a - gain.

2—Dis is de way I long have sought
Hard to rise again!
And mourned because I found it not.
Hard to rise again!

3—De debbil is a liar and a conjurer, too,
An' ef you don't mind he'll conjure you.

4—Oh, Satan he's a snake in de grass,
An' ef you don't mind, he'll git you at last.

One song is satisfied to snatch a single line from any convenient hymn, and pair it with one of its own in the refrain, while borrowing couplets right and left for the stanzas.

I WANT TO DIE A-SHOUTING.

2—Am I a soldier of the cross?
    I want to die a-shouting!
I want to feel my Saviour near,
    When soul and body's parting.
Must Jesus bear the cross alone?
    I want to die a-shouting!
No, there's a cross for every one,
    I want to die a-shouting!

3—Oh, Jesus loves the sinner-man,
    I want to die a-shouting!
I want to feel my Saviour near,
    When soul and body's parting.
I'm sometimes up and sometimes down,
    I want to die a-shouting!
But still my soul is Canaan bound,
    I want to die a-shouting!

4—Oh, sinners, turn, why will ye die?
    I want to die a-shouting!
I want to feel my Saviour near,
    When soul and body's parting.
Then here's my heart and here's my hand,
    I want to die a-shouting!
To meet you in the glory land
    I want to die a-shouting!

While the fitting together of couplets and refrains almost at random leads to some odd and incongruous combinations, upon the whole one is surprised to find with what good taste the mosaic is made, especially when the singing is led by an old-time leader with a wide range of couplets to choose from. Some of these men when confronted by an inquirer with notebook and pencil can hardly recall half a dozen of these stanzas; but in the fervor of their worship they not only remember them by the score, but by a sort of instinct rather than taste or judgment fit together words from different sources without a second's reflection or hesitation. It comes to pass sometimes that the words of a certain hymn attach themselves to a given refrain so that one rarely hears them separately. Here is one which I do not remember to have heard except with "Jerusalem, my happy home."

COMFORT IN HEAVEN.

While a majority of the negro melodies are in minor keys, the use of the major is far from being unusual, and is often very striking. A song called "Wake up, Children," is of this character. It is impossible to imagine a more appropriate musical setting for the opening words, or a clearer, heartier call to awaken.

WAKE UP, CHILDREN.

O wake up, chil-dren, wake up! O a-rise! O wake up, chil - dren, wake up! And I will serve that liv - ing God.

1. { Old Sa - tan tho't he had me fast, And I
{ But thank the Lord, I'm free at last, And I
will serve that liv - ing God.

2—Old Satan wears de hypocrite's shoe,
And I will serve that living God!
And if you don't mind he'll slip it on
to you,
And I will serve that living God!

The joys of heaven, prominent among which is its music, afford material for several songs.

I WANT TO GO WHERE JESUS IS.

REFRAIN.

I want to go where Je - sus is, To play up - on the gol - den harp,

To play up - on the gol - den harp, . . .

To play up - on the gol - den harp.

1. { Je - sus, my all, to heav'n is gone, To
{ He whom I fix my hopes up - on, To
play up - on the gol - den harp.

A good, ringing, hortatory hymn is entitled

COME ALONG.

REFRAIN.

Come a - long, come a - long, I am sor - ry for to leave you, On the road to heav-en, come, friends, will you go? I was but young when I be - gun, And now my race is near - ly run.

A cheerful song, with a strong major melody, is "Down by the River." The Baptists use it at immersion; but it is not confined to such occasions.

DOWN BY THE RIVER.

REFRAIN.

Yes, we'll gain this world, Down by the riv - er, We'll gain this world, Down by the riv - er-side.

1. And if those mourner's would be - lieve, Down by the riv-er, The gift of life they would re - ceive, Down by the riv-er-side.

2—When I was a mourner, just like you,
I mourned and mourned till I got through.

Many songs have a line three times repeated, with a fourth but little changed, and thus build a song out of meagre material; but the tunes are usually distinct. A very good one of this sort, and with a good tune, is

THE WINTER SOON BE OVER.

O the win - ter, the win - ter, the

win - ter soon be o - ver, chil - len,

The win - ter, the win - ter, the

win - ter soon be o - ver, chil - len,

The win - ter, the win - ter, the

win - ter soon be o - ver, chil - len,

And we'll all a - rise and go.

1. Them Metho-dists and Bap-tists can't a -

gree, And we'll all a - rise and go.

An' stop you long tongue from tell - ing

lies, And we'll all a - rise and go.

2—Oh, may I tell to sinners round
What a Saviour I have found.

3—Oh, may I tell to sisters all,
Stop your tongue from telling lies.

4—Sing glory, glory, glory to the Lamb,
I have held his bleeding hand.

I used sometimes to preach in a little church built by the colored people, the result of no small sacrifice and hard work. Besides the long Sunday services, held on stated Sundays once a month and whenever they had a preacher, they had innumerable night meetings at "early candle-lighting." For a bell they had a discarded circular saw from the sawmill, fastened to a tree before the door; and when I came in Uncle Joe would say: "Here comes Mistah Bahton now; I'll go out an' knock on de saw." The saw was a very good church bell, and brought the people straggling in from all about. We would spend some time singing while they gathered. The young people wanted book hymns, and had their way in part; but the older people were pleased that I liked the others, and I got many of them in written form. One that was often sung in those meetings was "Pray On." It is a hymn with a fixed refrain and variable stanzas, and is also a family hymn.

PRAY ON.

REFRAIN.

Pray on, broth-ers, O hal - ly - halle -

lu - jah! Pray on, broth - ers, It

1   V2 FINE.

ain't too late.   late. 1. I washed my

head   in the mid - night dew;

D.C.

The morn-ing stars a wit - ness, too.

2—If you get there before I do,
Just tell them I am coming too.

3—There grows a tree in Paradise,
The Christian calls it the tree of life.

There was a great revival in the to-bacco barn, and the meetings contin-ued late into the night. They were late in beginning, for those who at-tended were working people, and the "early candle-lighting" proved very late for a start. However, those who came first sang, and there was some-thing going on some nights from dusk till nearly daylight; for on the even-ings when there was a good benchful of tough old "mourners" who had been there once a year or so for a long time, there was a siege. The faithful called it "marching round Jericho," when, clearing the benches away, they marched round and round the mourn-ers' bench singing and stopping at in-tervals for prayer or to shout out, "Be-lieve, mourners!" Thomas Hughes, the genial author of "Tom Brown," was making his last visit to this coun-try at the time, and had never been at such a meeting. He made me a brief visit, and I took him there. He was a reverent and interested specta-tor, seeing the real spirit of worship that underlay some of the odd pro-ceedings, and also having an eye to all that was new to him in the situation.

During this long revival, which lasted a good many weeks, a bright young lady lay dying of consumption in the large house on the hill. As she lay at night near her open window she enjoyed hearing the colored peo-ple sing, and there was one hymn that touched her heart with its sweet-ness and pathos. As she felt her own time "drawing near" and began to lis-ten for the "charming bells," this hymn grew more dear to her; and as the colored people came to know that she cared for it, they grew accus-tomed to singing it each night, with all its stanzas, for her benefit.

Night after night I heard this song, —an invitation to the sinner, a glad anticipation of heaven, and a salute from the humble but kind hearted worshipers as they closed their meet-ing in the tobacco barn, to the dying girl in the big house on the hill, who listened nightly for this greeting.

DEM CHARMING BELLS.

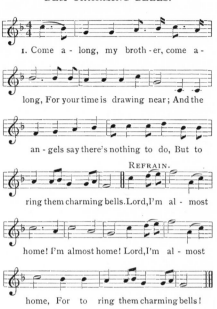

1. Come a - long, my broth - er, come a - long, For your time is drawing near; And the an - gels say there's nothing to do, But to

REFRAIN.

ring them charming bells. Lord, I'm al - most home! I'm almost home! Lord, I'm al - most home, For to ring them charming bells!

2—Come along, my sister, etc.

3—Come along, my preacher, etc.

4—Come along, my deacon, etc.

5—Come along, po' mourner, etc.

6—Come along, O sinner, etc.

7—Come along, Sister Mary, etc.

8—Come along, Sister Martha, etc.

9—Come along, Brother 'Lijah, etc.

10—Come along, true believer, etc.

As cold weather came on, she passed away, and we sent her body to the Northern home whence she had come too late. We had a simple little service in the chapel, and a company of the colored people sang the clear, bell-like notes of the song, which ever since has seemed to me most beauti-ful, with its ringing, confident, hope-ful and inspiring words,—

"Lord, I'm almost home,
    I'm almost home!
Lord, I'm almost home,
    For to ring dem charming bells."

The negro hymns seldom make allusion to the Bible as a source of inspiration. They prefer "heart religion" to "book religion." In some places where an ordinary hymn would strengthen assurance by a promise of God in Holy Scripture, the negro appeals to his own revelation from the Lord. The following hymn is an illustration:

WE'RE SOME OF THE PRAYING PEOPLE.

I have another Alabama hymn which, like the above, is made up of a threefold repetition and a concluding line.

The melody of this hymn starts in a way that reminds us of the Gospel Hymn, but when we come to the refrain we find the familiar swing and syncopation of the negro.

WEAR A STARRY CROWN.

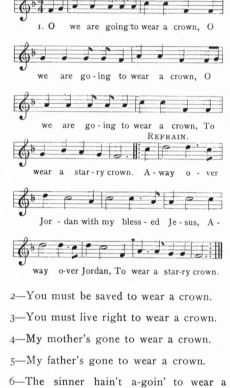

2—You must be saved to wear a crown.

3—You must live right to wear a crown.

4—My mother's gone to wear a crown.

5—My father's gone to wear a crown.

6—The sinner hain't a-goin' to wear a crown.

These hymns are fairly representative of a once numerous, but now vanishing class. Some are commonplace enough, both in words and music. But others glow with genuine religious fervor, and afford valuable material for a study of the social and religious life of the negro, besides being an important contribution to American folk lore.

HYMNS OF THE SLAVE AND THE FREEDMAN.

By William E. Barton, D. D.

I BEGAN my quest for quaint hymns when I was a school teacher, and was neither confined to a single place of worship nor prohibited by the responsibilities of my position from taking notes during service. After I began to preach I had more opportunities; but my field was somewhat restricted, and I was less sensitive to peculiarities which had impressed me in the earlier years of my residence in the South. I partially made my opportunities good, however, by visiting the older people who knew old songs, and writing these down as they sang them. One of my best friends in this regard was Aunt Dinah. It was from her I learned "Death's goner lay his cold icy hand on me;" and I fear that I could never have written it down had I not learned it from some one who would patiently repeat it again and again till I mastered its wonderful syncopations.

It is a peculiarity of the negro music that it can nearly all be swayed to and timed with the patting of the foot. No matter how irregular it appears to be, one who sways backward and forward and pats his foot finds the rhythm perfect. A young lady friend of mine was trying to learn some of the melodies from an old auntie, but found that the time as well as the tune baffled her. At length, when the old woman had turned to her work, the girl got to swaying and humming gently, patting her foot the while. The old woman turned and, patting the girl on the knee, said: "Dat's right, honey! Dat's de berry way! Now you's a-gittin' it, sho nuff! You'll nebbah larn 'em in de wuld till you sings dem in de sperrit!"

Now and then I would go to Aunt Dinah's cabin, and ask her for more songs. She invariably began by de-claring that I had long since learned all the songs she knew; but I would plead with her to cudgel her brains for some of the old ones, the ones they sang before the war. After the requisite amount of protesting, she would promise to think and see if she could remember any, but with the declaration that it was hopeless. "I'll go to de do' an' call Sistah Bemaugh," she would say, "an' we'll see ef we can't find some. An' while she's a-comin' ober, you se' down dah, an' I'll finish dis shirt."

I was fortunate to find her ironing, and wise enough not to propose songs if she were at the washtub. It was near a furlong across the hollow to Sister Bemaugh, and there was a sawmill between; but Aunt Dinah and Sister Bemaugh had no trouble about making themselves understood at this distance, and about the time Aunt Dinah had finished the shirt and set her irons down before the open fire, Sister Bemaugh was on hand. Then they both protested that they had sung me every song they knew, —and they invariably found one or two more. One of these songs was "Motherless Child," or "I feel like I'd never been borned." It is one of the most pathetic songs I ever heard.

Not very long ago I attended a concert given by a troupe of jubilee singers, whose leader was a member of the original Fisk company. Toward the end of the programme he announced that a recently arrived singer in his troupe from Mississippi had brought a song that her grandparents sang in slave times, which he counted the saddest and most beautiful of the songs of slavery. It was a mutilated version of Aunt Dinah's song; and it lacked the climax of the hymn as I have it,—the "Gi' down on my knees and pray, PRAY!" The swell on these words is indescribable. Its effect is almost physical. From the utter dejection of the first part it rises with a sustained, clear faith. It expresses more than the sorrows of slavery; it has also the deep religious nature of the slave, and the consolations afforded him in faith and prayer.

Sister Bemaugh did not know this song. Aunt Dinah explained it to her, as she learned it with me, and I wrote down many scraps of their conversation while they thought I was only writing down the hymn; and sometimes they talked for quite a while undisturbed by my presence, as I sat at the ironing-table beating out the tunes which they had sung. Said Aunt Dinah,—I copy from the margin of my score:

"You des' gotter staht dat song in a mourn. Dey hain't no uddah way to git de hang ub it. Fus' time I hear it, I wis' de Lawd I cud lun it. I tried an' tried, an' couldn't. I went home studyin' it, an' all to once it come a-ringin' through me. Den I sung it all night."

The stanzas are double, and the two halves are sung to the same tune.

MOTHERLESS CHILD.

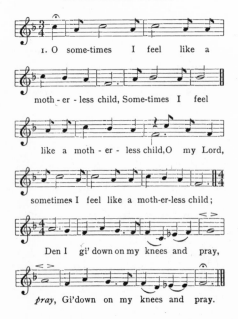

1. O some-times I feel like a moth - er - less child, Some-times I feel like a moth - er - less child, O my Lord, sometimes I feel like a moth-er-less child;

Den I gi' down on my knees and pray,

pray, Gi'down on my knees and pray.

1—O, sometimes I feel like a motherless child!
Sometimes I feel like a motherless child!
    O my Lord!
Sometimes I feel like a motherless child!
Den I git down on my knees and pray, pray!
Git down on my knees and pray!
O, I wonder where my mother's done gone,
Wonder where my mother's done gone,
I wonder where my mother's done gone.
Den I git down on my knees and pray, pray!
Git down on my knees and pray!

2—O, sometimes I feel like I'd never been borned,
Sometimes I feel like I'd never been borned,
    O my Lord!
Sometimes I feel like I'd never been borned,
Den I git down on my knees and pray, pray!
Git down on my knees and pray!
O, I wonder where my baby's done gone,
Wonder where my baby's done gone,
Wonder where my baby's done gone.
Den I git down on my knees and pray, pray!
Git down on my knees and pray!

3—O, sometimes I feel like I'm a long ways from home, etc.
I wonder where my sister's done gone, etc.

4—Sometimes I feel like a home-e-less child, etc.
I wonder where de preacher's done gone, etc.

Sister Bemaugh had not sung so much in church since the visit of the singing brother during the revival, to which I referred in my previous article. Proud as she felt of the fact that they had had to call on her at the end to start a song, she felt sore about the prominence of the strange singing brother that one night, and my effort to learn from her some of the songs which he had sung was futile. They were "no 'count songs," anyway, she thought. While I was writing down another song, I overheard a conversation between her and Aunt Dinah, and wrote down a scrap of it, which

I quote verbatim from the corner of the sheet where I then wrote it.

Quoth Sister Bemaugh to Aunt Dinah: "Does you know why I doesn't sing in church no mo'? Dey hain't used to my voice."

To which Aunt Dinah replied: "Don' you wait for dat. You voice all right. You kin sing des' like a parrot."

Their conversation developed the fact that Aunt Dinah knew one of the most fetching songs which the visitor had sung, and she offered to sing it for me, taking pains to save Sister Bemaugh's feelings. It appeared later that Sister Bemaugh knew it also, though she would not sing it with him. She sang it with Aunt Dinah, however, when it was once started,— and I got it all. One of the quaint things about it is the expression, "Gwineter argue wid de Father and chatter wid de Son." I had often heard the expression, "Gwineter chatter wid de angels," in these songs, but this expression was new to me. "Argue," as here employed, does not mean dispute, but only to converse learnedly; and "chatter" does not imply frivolity, but only familiarity. The underlying theology has always seemed to me interesting.

2—I never can forget the day
When Jesus washed my sins away.

3—Gwine to argue wid de Father and chatter wid de Son,
Gwine talk 'bout de bright world dey des' come from.

4—When Jesus shuck de manna tree,
He shuck it for you, an' he shuck it for me.

5—De trumpet shall sound, an' de dead shall rise,
And go to mansions in de skies.

6—Of all de folks I like de bes'
I love de shouting Methodist.

Both Sister Bemaugh and Aunt Dinah agreed that the church to which they belonged was cold, and sometimes they had to provoke each other to love and good works in view of its depressing influence upon them. It never seemed cold when I was there, but they agreed that by the time meeting would get fairly to going here, their respective home churches would have been "all in a mourn." Aunt Dinah complained (I copy again from the margin of my score):

"Dis chu'ch powerful cold. It des' scrunches me. It's so indifferent from our home chu'ch. Sometimes I goes dah, an I feels de Sperrit, but I hangs my head and squenches it. I knows I'se changed from nature to grace, but when I goes dah, I don' feel like I'se gone to chu'ch. It ain't like it used to be wid me at home. De Sperrit has lifted me right up. I'se shouted dah much as I please, and sometimes I'se des' sot dah an' tickled myself, and den agin I've mighty nigh hugged Sistah Williams to death!"

To this Sister Bemaugh would respond: "When you feels de Sperrit, you mustn't squench him."

Perhaps the next time the complaint and exhortation would be reversed. Anyway, they agreed in their declaration that the church was not what it ought to be, and they sometimes grew almost ecstatic as they hummed and gossiped in the chimney corner while I wrote at the ironing table.

I'LL BE THERE.

REFRAIN.

For I'll be there, ... For I'll be there,

I'll be there, I'll be there, When the last FINE.

trum-pet shall sound, I'll be there.

{ An' if those mourners would be-lieve, The
{ The gift of life they would re-ceive, The
D.C.

last trumpet shall sound, I'll be there.

One of Aunt Dinah's hymns was "The heaven bells ringin'" and I'm a-goin' home," which was sung to a ringing tune. It requires but little imagination to hear the ringing of bells to its "going, going home." I have heard the same words sung to another tune, but the ring of this one is remarkable.

HEAVEN BELLS RINGIN', AND I'M A-GOIN' HOME.

O de heav'n bells a - ring - in', and I'm a-go-in', go - in' home; De heav'n bells a - ring-in', and I'm a - go-in', go - in' home; De heaven bells a - ring - in', and I'm a - go - in', go-in' home, a-climb-in' up Zi-on's hill.

2—De heaven bells ringin', an' my mother's goin', goin' home, etc.

3—De heaven bells ringin', and my Jesus goin', goin' home, etc.

4—De heaven bells ringin', and de sinner's lost, he's lost a home, etc.

Another of Aunt Dinah's songs was "Mighty Day." The refrain is a four-fold repetition of the question, "O wasn't that a mighty day?"—but this is usually repeated so as to make eight repetitions. The verses follow more or less closely the events of the Apocalypse, and are of variable length.

In their fondness for eschatology, and the joy with which they anticipate the day of judgment and dwell upon its terrific and sublime features, the hymns are a fair echo and antiphon of the preaching which they accompany.

MIGHTY DAY.

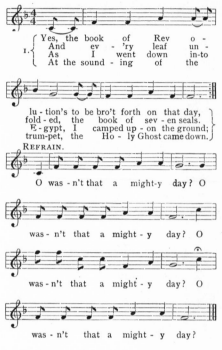

Yes, the book of Rev o-
And ev - 'ry leaf un-
As I went down in-to
At the sound - ing of the

lu - tion's to be bro't forth on that day,
fold - ed, the book of sev - en seals.
E - gypt, I camped up - on the ground;
trum-pet, the Ho - ly Ghost came down.

REFRAIN.

O was - n't that a might-y day? O was - n't that a might - y day? O was - n't that a might - y day? O was - n't that a might - y day?

2—And when the seals was opened,
  The voice said, "Come and see,"
I went and stood a-looking
  To see the mystery.
The red horse came a-galloping,
  And the black horse he came, too,
And the pale horse he came down the road,
  And stole my father away.

Refrain.

3—And then I seen old Satan,
  And they bound him with a chain,
And they put him in the fi-ar,
  And I seen the smoke arising.
They bound him in the fi-ar,
  Where he wanted to take my soul,
Old Satan gnashed his teeth and howled,
  And missed po' sinner man's soul.

Refrain.

4—Then I see the dead arisin',
  And stand before the Lamb,
And the wicked calls on the mountains
  To hide them from His face.
And then I see the Christian
  A-standin' on the right hand of Jesus,
And a-shoutin' Hallelujah,
  Singin' praises to the Lamb.

5—I bless de Lord I'm goin' to die,
  I'm goin' to judgment by and by.

Another hymn which I heard both at Aunt Dinah's fireside and in meetings was "Anybody Here." Anyone who cares to sing it will recognize in the melody of the second half a strain so decidedly like the Scotch that he might well wed it to one of Burns's poems. The resemblance is apparent, not only in the slurring, hopping effect which almost matches that in "Within a Mile of Edinboro' Town," but also in the threefold repetition of the final tonic note.

ANYBODY HERE?

REFRAIN.
Is there an - y-bod-y here That loves my Je - sus? An-y-bod-y here that loves my Lord? O, I want to know if you love my Je - sus; FINE. I want to know if you love my Lord. 1. The an - gel's wings were tipp'd with D.C. gold, That bro't sal - va-tion to my soul.

2—What kind of shoes is them you wear,
   That you may walk upon the air?

3—This world 's a wilderness of woe,
   Let us all to glory go.

4—I do believe without a doubt
   That a Christian has a right to shout.

5—Religion is a blooming rose,
   As none but them that feels it knows.

6—You say you're aiming for the skies;
   Why don't you stop your telling lies?

7—When every star refuse to shine,
   I know King Jesus will be mine.

It was in connection with the song, "Rule Death in His Arms," that I heard Aunt Dinah tell her religious experience to Sister Bemaugh. She was only a little girl, she said, when the war broke out,—"jes' a water-toter." That was as nearly as she could estimate her age, that at the outbreak of hostilities she was large enough to "tote water" to the men in the field. Her uncle, she said, was taken with other slaves to erect fortifications in Virginia before the time when colored troops were allowed to enlist, and while at that work was shot. She saw him while he was dying, and said to him, "You'd better pray;" but he cursed her and said, "I done got past prayin';" and she added, "An' right den he died." She continued the narrative with a good deal of awe, but with no special exhibition of concern for her uncle. Said she: "Dat night I seed him. An' he was in dat ba-a-ad place! An' de debbil des' a-shovin' fire on him wid a pitch-fork! Yeas, ma'am! De debbil has got a pitch-fork! I seed him! An' one club foot! An' my uncle looked up an' seed me. An' I says, 'Aha! You'd orter prayed when I tole you!' An' he says, 'I wish de Lawd I had a-prayed!' Dat's what he said. Sesee, 'You needn't nebbah want to come heah!' An' I says, 'I hain't a-comin' dah, now you des' see!' An' den de ole debbil looked up, an' he says, 'Yes, an' I'm a-comin' to git you bime-by.' An' den I looked, an' I couldn't see what I was a-stannin' on, an' I was right over it. Mus' 'a' been de power of God dat kep' me from fallin' in. An' den I begun to pray. O, but I had a hard time a-gittin' through! I reckon de Lawd mos' made up His mind not to wash away my sins, 'cause I danced so much! But bime-by I learn dis song; and when I learn dat song, de Lawd spoke peace to my soul."

The song is a chant with very irregular lines and a refrain. The figure, "Rule death in his arms," is, I suppose, that of a parent subduing an unruly child. It is almost impossible to write this tune. Even the selection of a key is difficult. It runs an octave below its keynote, and while the range above is only five notes, it is common to sing the "sinner" verse an octave higher, thus covering two octaves and a third. The time, also, varies in the different stanzas, but with the same cadences. The value of this melody is almost wholly in the expression given to it. The notes alone are colorless.

RULE DEATH IN HIS ARMS.

2—See the sinnah lyin' on his deathbed,
An' a Death come a-steppin' in;
You heah the sinnah say to Death,
"Let me pray God for my sin!"
An' you heah Death say to the sinnah,
"You been heah long enough to pray
God for you sin."

3—Yes, you heah Death say to the sinnah-
man,
"You been heah long enough to pray
God for you sin."
God Almighty has sent me heah for
you,
An' I can't let you stay."

4—When God commanded Gabriel
To blow the silver trumpet,
He called the living to judgment,
And the dead come forth from the
grave.

5—See the Christian lyin' on his death-
bed,
An' a Death come a-steppin' in;
You heah dat Christian say to Death,
"O Death, you are welcome."

Sister Bemaugh and Aunt Dinah sang this over and over while I was writing it down, first for my benefit and then for their own enjoyment.

I have other songs which I learned from these two good old women, some of them used before and others to follow in this paper. The songs obtained from them were unadulterated by book-religion or any modern tinkering. Every quaver, every slur, every syncopation was there, and I took the greatest pains to write them as they gave them. There was one which they called "De Coffin to Bind Me Down." They made a very long song of it by using the verses again and again, the first line in one verse serving as the third in another, and coupled with a different companion. There were only four lines and the refrain, "De coffin to bind me down;" but out of these they made certainly four times four stanzas.

THE COFFIN TO BIND ME DOWN.

2—To dust, to dust, to dust we go,
    De coffin to bind me down!
    A golden chain to let me down,
    De coffin to bind me down!

De coffin to bind me down!
De coffin to bind me down!
A folding sheet upon my lips,
De coffin to bind me down!

Besides making a very respectable hymn out of a few lines, these two women could make a reasonably good tune out of three or four notes. I have heard them sing one which I could hardly believe had so small a compass till I came to write it and found that it was all covered by the first three notes of the scale, *do, re, mi.* Such a song is: "I don't want you go on and leave me." It is a pathetic little hymn.

I DON'T WANT YOU GO ON AND
LEAVE ME.

The singer is toddling along with short and broken steps, trying to keep in sight of the Lord, and pleading not to be left behind.

The negroes have many hymns of the "Old Ship of Zion." The talented young southern poet, Irwin Russell, gave an exceedingly funny description of the ark as interpreted in the light of a negro's experience with a river steamer. Such anachronisms sometimes work themselves in perfect good faith into these hymns. But the hymn of this sort which I liked best was one which I learned from Aunt Dinah. The ring and swing of the refrain, "I'm no ways weary," are truly inspiring. I used frequently to hum it on my long mountain rides till there came some measure of relief from fatigue from its buoyant spirit.

THE OLD SHIP OF ZION.

2—She has landed many thousands, Hallelujah!

3—King Jesus is her captain, Hallejuh!

4—O, get your ticket ready, Hallelujah!

5—She is coming in the harbor, Hallelujah!

6—She will land you safe in heaven, Hallelujah!

7—She will never rock nor totter, Hallelujah!

Some of the old slave songs survive which had in them the bitterness of a sorrow that never spoke its intensity in plain words, but sought figures from the Bible or veiled its real meaning in inarticulate moans or songs of grief that never uttered the real nature of the sorrow. Yet every minor note was the wail of a broken heart, and every syncopation the snapping of a heartstring. One of these is called "Po' Me."

PO' ME!

REFRAIN.   *ad lib.*

Why, breth-er-ing,   Po' me! Po' me!
Why, sis-ter-ing,

tempo.   *ad lib.*

Trouble will bur-y me down! Po' me!

tempo.

Po' me! Trouble will bur-y me down!

2—Hallelujah once, hallelujah twice,
  Trouble will bury me down!
  De Lawd is on de giving hand,
  Trouble will bury me down!

Refrain.

  Why, sistering,
  Po' me! Po' me!
  Trouble will bury me down!
  Po' me! Po' me!
  Trouble will bury me down!

3—Sometimes I think I'm ready to drop,
  Trouble will bury me down!
  But, thank de Lawd, I do not stop,
  Trouble will bury me down!

Refrain.

But, O my Lawd,
  Po' me! Po' me!
Trouble will bury me down!
  Po' me! Po' me!
Trouble will bury me down!

One of the most pathetic of all these songs, its minor strains the very acme of sorrow, is "Troubled in Mind." I think that it has been printed, but neither words nor music are as I have heard them.

TROUBLED IN MIND.

1. In the morn-ing I am trou-bled

Fo' day! I am troubled in mind! mind!

2—While I'se walkin' I am troubled,
    All day!
  I am troubled in mind.

3—O sinnah, I am troubled!
    All day!
  I am troubled in mind.

4—O my Jesus, I am troubled!
    All day!
  I am troubled in mind.

The direct references to slavery in the negro songs are surprisingly few. Probably few of the people had come to think of slavery itself as abnormal or of its hardships as justly chargeable to the system; and it is still more probable that the grief which they felt they were constrained to veil behind general lamentation without speaking plainly the sorrows which they regarded as inevitable.

It is noteworthy that these songs, however much they bewail the sorrows of slavery, contain no resentment. The only known exception, if it be an exception, is the joy over the fact that

"When Moses smote the water,
The waters came together
And drowned old Pharaoh's army. Hallelu!"

The secular songs of freedom, "De Massa Run," "Babylon is Fallen," "Bobolishion's Comin'" and the rest, are tolerably familiar. But there is one hymn which I used often to hear which speaks the freedman's joy in his new manhood. I have heard it sung sometimes in the North by companies of educated jubilee singers, who introduce it with the lines,

"Holy Bible! Holy Bible!
Holy Bible, Book Divine, Book Divine!"

But I never heard these words sung as a verse of this or any native plantation hymn in the South. Their references to the Bible are few, and such as are given in the songs of this series, namely, allusions to well-known narrative portions of Scripture. The "Holy Bible" stanza was probably the addition of some "reading preacher." It is quite as appropriate, however, as those which are sung to the song in the South; for the freedman, preferring death to slavery, and singing his solemn joy in a strong and stirring strain, comforts himself in the thought of the possibility of death, with the details of the first-class funeral, in which he is to play the chief rôle. Such a funeral as is described in this hymn is, next to heaven, the desire of the average colored man even in a state of grace. But apart from all this, which may provoke a smile, there is something that thrills one in the words:

"Before I'd be a slave,
I'd be buried in my grave,
And go home to my Lord and be saved!"

BEFORE I'D BE A SLAVE.

Be-fore I'd be a slave, I'd be buried in my grave, And go home to my Lord and be saved.

1. O, what preachin'! O, what preachin'!
O, what preachin' o-ver me, o-ver me!

2—O, what mourning, etc.

3—O, what singing, etc.

4—O, what shouting, etc.

5—O, weeping Mary, etc.

6—Doubting Thomas, etc.

7—O, what sighing, etc.

As I write the words of this hymn I seem to hear old Uncle Joe Williams sing them. Slavery had not been unkind to him. He always hired his time from his master and made money enough to pay for his labor, and had a good start toward buying his wife and children when freedom came. But this is the hymn he loved to sing, sitting before his door in the twilight.

For the most part the war did little for negro song. The melodies which are most characteristic gain little from association with outside influences. But here and there we may trace in words or music a theme which the war suggested and which is worth noting. Choicest among these specimens is "Sinner, You'd Better Get Ready." In several ways it seems a departure from ordinary negro music, but it is quite characteristic. It is in triple time; it is major; and the melody of the refrain, which is its more important part, is entirely in thirds, unless we take account of the three notes before the last one, which as now sung make a slight variation, but which are easily changed to conform to the rule. As written, the lower notes are as sung; the upper harmony is as it would be played. With this slight change it can be played on a keyless bugle.

SINNER, YOU BETTER GET READY.

Sin - ner, you bet - ter get read - y,

Sin - ner, you bet - ter get read - y,

Sin -ner, you bet - ter get read - y, For the

FINE.

hour is a - com - in' Dat a sin- ner must die.

1. { The tall - est tree in Par - a - dise,
The Chris-tian calls it the tree of life,

D.C.

Hour is a com-in' Dat a sin - ner must die.

2—I looked at my hands, my hands was new;
I looked at my feet, my feet was, too.

3—My name's written in de book of life,
If you look in de book you'll find it there.

4—De good old chariot passing by,
She jarred the earth and shook the sky.

Another song that uses almost wholly the open notes is "Little David, Play on Your Harp." It is less like a bugle song than "Sinner, You Better Get Ready," but it is striking in its use of major thirds and fifths, the more so as, following the negro predilection for minor beginnings, this decidedly major tune starts on *la*. Its opening notes are, *la sol do mi do, la sol do, do do mi, do mi sol.*

LITTLE DAVID, PLAY ON YOUR HARP.

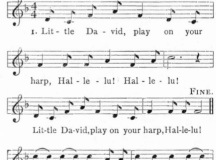

1. Lit - tle Da - vid, play on your

harp, Hal - le - lu! Hal - le - lu!

FINE.

Lit-tle Da-vid, play on your harp, Hal-le-lu!

1. Lit-tle David was a shepherd boy; He
2. Josh - u-a was the son of Nun; He
3. Jes' wait till I get on the mountain top; Gwine to

D.C.

killed Go - li -ath, and he shout-ed for joy!
nev-er did stop till his work was done.
make my wings go flip - pi - ty flop.

4—Peter walked upon the sea,
And Jesus told him, "Come to me."

5—Elijah slew the prophets of Baal;
The rain came down and did not fail.

6—If you belong to Gideon's band,
Then here's my heart and here's my hand.

7—They cast Brer Jonah overboard,
And a big whale swallowed Brer Jonah whole.

If the foregoing suggest a bugle, not less so do some others suggest the tap of the drum. There is no better example than one lately given me by Rev. George W. Moore, field missionary of the American Missionary Association, and husband of one of the original jubilee singers, whose voice still is often heard at annual meetings of that association. Anyone who will for a moment disregard the tones, and tap the notes or sing them in monotone with a rat-tat-a-tat, will see that the time of the song "I'm Goin' to Sing" is such as might well have been derived from the beat of an army drum.

I'M GOIN' TO SING.

O I'm goin' to sing, Goin' to

sing, Goin' to sing, Goin' to

sing all a - long my way.

O I'm goin' to sing, Goin' to

sing, Goin' to sing, Goin' to

FINE.

sing all a - long my way.

1. We want no cow-ards in our band, Who
2. Are there no foes for me to face, Must

will their col-ors fly; We call for val-iant
I not stem the flood? Is this vile world a

D.C.

heart - ed men Who're not a - fraid to die.
friend to grace, To help me on to God?

Some of these war songs are exceedingly simple in structure, often having only a single line that can be called a permanent part of the hymn. This is often repeated, sometimes shortened, and again lengthened by a hortatory ejaculation or a direct address; but the rest of the hymn is built up as occasion demands,—and in some cases the one line, or germ cell of the song, is found to vary greatly in different versions. Sometimes a single couplet attaches itself to the refrain in such a way as to be commonly recognized as the first stanza, but for the rest the song hunts about for couplets from "Jesus, My All," or other hymns with lines of the same length. Some of these, however, are rather effective.

STAY IN THE FIELD.

REFRAIN.

O stay in the field, chil-der-en-ah

Stay in the field, chil-der-en-ah,

FINE.

Stay in the field, Un-til the war is end-ed

1. {I've got my breastplate, sword, and shield,
   And I'll go march-ing thro' the field,

D.C.

Till the war is end - ed.

2—Satan thought he had me fast,
    Till the war is ended;
    But thank the Lord I'm free at last,
    Till the war is ended.

No other couplet of this as I learned it has any military suggestion. The other verses used are such as are given in the songs with constant refrains and variable stanzas.

There are several simple songs that fit a military pledge of fealty to familiar words, with a simple but effective tune, as:

SOLDIER FOR JESUS.

REFRAIN.

1. I'm a sol - dier for Je - sus, En-

list - ed for the war, And I'll fight un -

FINE.

til I die. 1. Am . . I a

sol - dier of the cross, And

D.C.

shall I fear to own His cause.

2—This is the way I long have sought
And mourned because I found it not.

3—I've got my breastplate, sword and shield,
And I will die upon the field.

There are suggestions of enlistment in songs about joining the band. The allusions are generally indefinite, but such as might well come from a general suggestion of military figures adapted for use in worship.

GWINE TER JINE DE BAND.

1. Haint but one thing that grieves my mind,
Band of an - gels leaves me be-hind—ah!

3—Swing low, chariot, pillar in de East,
All God's chillen gwine ter hab a little feast—ah!

4—Swing low, chariot, pillar in de West,
All God's chillen gwine ter hab a little rest—ah!

5—Swing low, chariot, pillar in the South,
All God's chillen gwine ter hab a little shout—ah!

Each stanza of the above hymn ends with a euphonic Ah! which connects it with and merges into the refrain. A like syllable is used at the end of the second line of the refrain.

Now and then the word "Union," pronounced in three syllables, is added to the "band," and may indi-

cate yet more plainly the army origin of some of these songs. One of these is:

STAND ON A SEA OF GLASS.

1. { Sa - tan tried my soul to slay
{ Sword of faith skeered him a - way,
Stand on a sea of glass.

2—When Jesus shook the manna tree,—
Stand on a sea of glass,
He shook it for you and shook it for me,—
Stand on a sea of glass,

3—Talles' tree in Paradise,—
Stand on a sea of glass,
Christian calls it de tree of life,—
Stand on a sea of glass,

The negro pronunciation of "This Union" was said to be turned to good account by certain merchants living in the border states during the war, among whom a popular placard bore a picture of a contraband throwing up his hat and shouting, "Dis Union Forever!" The words were so spaced as to leave the phrase beautifully ambiguous, and it was explained as "This Union forever," or "Disunion forever," according to the exigencies of the occasion.

Another version, with a different tune, is found in a grouping of the "Union band" with that theme of perpetual interest and ecstatic contemplation, the big camp meeting in the promised land. There are many songs that dwell on the last of these, and some that combine the two.

BIG CAMP MEETING IN THE PROMISED LAND.

O dis un - i - on! O dis

un - i - on band! O dis un - i - on!

FINE.

Big camp meeting in de prom-ised land!

1. { You kin hinder me here, but you can't do it there,
{ For He sits in de heavens, and He answers prayer,

D.C.

Big camp meeting in de promised land!

2—I hain't got time for to stop an' talk,
De road is rough and it's hard to walk.

I have one song that seems to be made up from an army march tune and the two hymns, "All Hail the Power" and "Am I a Soldier of the Cross?"

CROWND HIM LORD OF ALL.

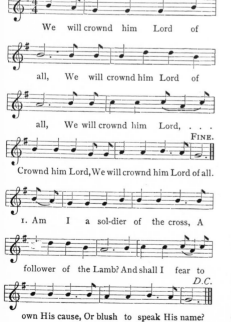

REFRAIN.

We will crownd him Lord of

all, We will crownd him Lord of

all, We will crownd him Lord, . . .

FINE.

Crownd him Lord, We will crownd him Lord of all.

1. Am I a sol-dier of the cross, A

follower of the Lamb? And shall I fear to

D.C.

own His cause, Or blush to speak His name?

One feature of army life impressed the negro deeply. It was the calling of the roll and the lining up of the men to answer to their names. It has its echoes in several hymns, some of which have been published; but the most striking one which I have ever heard I give below:

WHEN THAT GENERAL ROLL IS CALLED.

REFRAIN.

I'll be there in the morning, I'll be

there in . the morn-ing, I'll be

there in the morn - ing, When that

gen-er-al roll is called, I'll be there, When that

gen-er-al roll is called, I'll be there.

1. Gwine to see my father, I'll be there; Gwine to

1   2 D.C.

see my fa-ther, I'll be there; Gwine to there.

2—Goin' to see my mother, etc.

3—Goin' to see my sister, etc.

4—Goin' to see my brother, etc.

5—Goin' to see my Jesus, etc.

These are quite enough to illustrate the effect of the war upon the songs of the negro, and are the principal hymns of this kind which have come to my notice.

These retain, for the most part, the genuine negro characteristics, but illustrate the imitative bent of the negro mind, and manifest more or less distinctly outside influences.

There is an element of religious selfishness in some of these songs and a rejoicing in the relative exclusiveness of religion as the singers understand it. We have noticed it already in such couplets as:

"Wait till I get in the middle of the air,
There won't be nary sinner there."

It constitutes the burden of some songs. I do not know that it is more pronounced in these than in some more pretentious hymns. I hear quite often in evangelistic meetings a song of heaven in which, as I first heard it, the words were:

"I shall know Him, I shall know Him,
And alone by His side I shall stand,
I shall know Him, I shall know Him,
By the print of the nails in His hand."

Such songs are as open to criticism on the ground either of an unspiritual materialism or of a religious self-seeking as are any of the negro hymns. Recently, however, I have heard this one sung, "And *redeemed* by His side I shall stand," which eliminates one objectionable feature.

The hymn which I give as illustrating this characteristic is "I'm Going to Walk with Jesus by Myself." The tune is much the same as that of "Who Will Drive the Chariot When She Comes?" And this reminds me that many of these tunes that seem monotonously alike when written, have a much wider variety when sung to different words and with the *ad libitum* of the negro singer. In this the melodies are much like those of Scotland. Who ever would have known by ear alone that the tune of "I'm wearin' awa, John," is the very same as that of "Scots wha hae wi' Wallace bled"? And for that matter, who, knowing the pathetic sweetness of the one and the martial solemnity of the other, would have suspected that both these airs are simply the silly old ditty of "Hey, tuttie, tattie"? Even so these negro melodies are not to be too lightly scorned because of their monotony, which is often more apparent than real.

I'M GOIN' TO WALK WITH JESUS
BY MYSELF.

1. I am goin' to walk with Je-sus by my-
2. I'm goin' to talk with Je-sus by my-
3. I'm goin' to see King Je-sus by my-
4. I'm goin' to live with Je-sus by my-

self, by my-self, I am goin' to walk with
self, by my-self, I am goin' to talk with
self, by my-self, I am goin' to see King
self, by my-self, I am goin' to live with

Je-sus by my-self, by my-self, I'm
Je-sus by my-self, by my-self, I'm
Je-sus by my-self, by my-self, I'm
Je-sus by my-self, by my-self, I'm

goin' to walk with Je-sus, I'm
goin' to talk with Je-sus, I'm
goin' to see King Je-sus, I'm
goin' to live with Je-sus, I'm

goin' to walk with Je-sus, I'm
goin' to talk with Je-sus, I'm
goin' to see King Je-sus, I'm
goin' to live with Je-sus, I'm

goin' to walk with Je-sus by my-self.
goin' to talk with Je-sus by my-self.
goin' to see King Je-sus by my-self.
goin' to live with Je-sus by my-self.

A good many of the hymns of the colored people deal with ecstatic experiences; but most of them are sufficiently modest in their claims of regenerate character and of fruits meet for repentance. Now and then, however, there is a song whose singer professes to have received sanctification. It has been my privilege to know a number of people, white and black, who were thought by others to be sanctified in the sense in which that term is commonly (and incorrectly) used; but these people always denied it. On the other hand, I have known a number of people who thought themselves to be sanctified, and in no case could any one else be made to believe it. However, here is the hymn, which is rather a rare one of its sort.

It may be noted that while conversion implies a long struggle to "get through," sanctification, as here interpreted, is not related to antecedent experience. It occurs simply while "walking along."

DONE BEEN SANCTIFIED.

1. One day I'se a-walk-ing a-long, The Lord done sanc-ti-fied me;
One day I'se walk-ing a-long, He sanc-ti-fied my soul.
Sin-ner, be-hold the Lamb of God, The Lord done sanc-ti-fied me;
Sin-ner, be-hold the Lamb of God. He sanc-ti-fied my soul.

1—One day I'se walkin' along,
  The Lord done sanctified me.
One day I'se walkin' along,
  He sanctified my soul.
Mourner, behold de Lamb of God,
  The Lord done sanctified me.
He sanctified me, he'll sanctify you,
  He sanctified my soul.

2—I went to the valley to pray,
  The Lord done sanctified me;
I climbed to the mountain top,
  He sanctified my soul.
Sinner, behold de Lamb, etc.

3—Before I learned to pray,
  The Lord done sanctified me;
I'd trouble all the day,
  He sanctified my soul.
Brother, behold the Lamb of God, etc.

4—I'se lost and now I'm found,
  The Lord done sanctified me;
My soul is heaven bound,
  He sanctified my soul.
Preachers, behold the Lamb of God,
  etc.

A good old hymn is "Don't you want to go?" I count it one of the gems of negro song.

DON'T YOU WANT TO GO?

1. O broth-er, don't you want to go?
2. O sis-ter, don't you want to go?
3. O sin-ner, don't you want to go?

O broth-er, don't you want to go?
O sis-ter, don't you want to go?
O sin-ner, don't you want to go?

O broth-er, don't you want to go? Come,
O sis-ter, don't you want to go? Come,
O sin-ner, don't you want to go? Come,

less go down to Jor-dan, Hal-le-lu!

REFRAIN.

Less go down to Jor-dan! Less go down to Jor-dan! Less go down to Jor-dan, Hal-le-lu---jah!.

Less go down to Jor-dan! Less go down to Jordan! Less go down to Jordan, Hal-le-lu!

Jordan and the sea furnish abundant figures for these songs; and the river applies equally well to baptism or to death.. One of these songs is, "You can't cross here." It is a dialogue, and a warning to the sinner who will one day attempt to cross where he will not be able.

This brings us around again to the theme of the resurrection, which always suggests a song. This time it may as well be, "Dese bones gwine ter rise again." Sometimes family names are interjected before the third "I know," and varied.

YOU CAN'T CROSS HERE.

O where you go-ing, sin-ner? O
where you go-ing, I say? Go-ing
down to the riv-ers of Jor-dan, You
can't cross here. 1. Yes, you must have that
true re-li-gion, Yes, you must have that
true re-li-gion, Yes, you must have that
true re-li-gion, Or you can't cross here.

2—Lord, I'm so glad my soul's converted,
Lord, I'm so glad my soul's converted,
Lord, I'm so glad my soul's converted,
You can't cross here.

3—I'm so glad my soul's converted,
I'm so glad I've got religion;
Yes, I'm going down to Jurdin,
You can't cross here.

4—I'm so glad that Jesus loves me,
I'm so glad I'm going to heaven,
I'm so glad my soul's converted,
You can't cross here.

THESE BONES GWINETER RISE AGAIN.

I know, I know, my Lord, I
know These bones gwine-ter rise a-gain.

Heav-en is a high and a loft-y place,
But you can't get there if you haint got the grace,
These bones gwine-ter rise a-gain.

2—Little did I think dat he was so nigh;
Dese bones gwineter rise again;
Spoke, and he made me laugh and cry;
Dese bones gwineter rise again.

3—When Gabriel makes his trumpet sound,
De saints shall rise and bust de ground.

4—You kin hender me here, but you can't do it dah,
For he sits in de heavens and he answers prah,

With this good old hymn, I bring this paper to a close. It is a fitting one for a finale. It is irregular in its composition, but with a flowing metre and with phrases of equal length as measured, though wedded to lines of two, four, seven, ten and more syllables. It has the characteristic introductory refrain and the monotonous croon for the couplet and response. It has also the clear faith, the fondness for the supernatural and the joyous conception of the Christian life common to these songs.

NOTE. Dr. Barton's first paper was published in the NEW ENGLAND MAGAZINE for December, 1898. A third and final paper will appear in the February number. So large a collection of these songs has not, we believe, appeared outside the Fisk and Hampton collections, and the total is nearly equal to either of those books.—EDITOR.

RECENT NEGRO MELODIES.

By William E. Barton, D. D.

IN two previous articles I have given fifty-four old plantation hymns, including both those of unquestioned antiquity and those which show the influence of the war and the effects of newly found freedom. In the present paper I propose to consider some which show more recent influences.

I cannot pretend, however, that the classification which I have made is strictly chronological. Material is lacking for a hard and fast division of these songs into historical groups. A song which I have recently learned, and which the man who sang it for me assured me was composed by a man well known to him, has all the characteristics of the older melodies. I have selected, in part, the songs that had common or contrasting features in melody or doctrine, and I shall include in this article some songs that were simply left over from the preceding ones. And the so-called "railroad songs" which make up a part of this article, though in their present form modern, represent a very old type of hymn structure, and had their beginnings far back in the days of slavery. No one man made them, nor are they ever written or ever complete. But I have endeavored to follow the general principle of grouping these songs according to their probable age.

Beside the "railroad songs" proper, there are some that are about the railroad. One of these will illustrate how modern influences in the South have affected the content of negro hymns.

To the negro on the levee the steamboat is the greatest thing afloat. But to the negro of the interior the place of the steamer in religious typology is assigned to the locomotive. There are several songs about the Gospel Train, some of which are familiar. The railroad seems so supernatural that it is hard to convince some faithful old souls that heaven is not at one or the other terminus. There is a good old song with this suggestion. It is in triple time, and pronounces "evening" in three sharp syllables.

GIT ON THE EVENING TRAIN.

Gwine to git on de e - ven -ing train, train,

Git on de e - ven - ing train. O train.

Git on de e - ven -ing train, train, my Lord,

Git on de e - ven - ing train.

O, how do you know, know, O how do you

know, O, know, O, how do you know,

know, my Lord, O, . . how do you know?

My Lord told - a me so, so,
1. Ga - briel's trumpet shall blow, blow,

My Lord told - a me so, O so,
Ga - briel's trumpet shall blow, O blow,

My Lord told - a me so, So, my Lord,
Ga-briel's trumpet shall blow, Blow, my Lord,

My Lord told - a me so.
Ga - briel's trum-pet shall blow.

33

2—Old Death stayin' in de grave, grave,
etc.

3—Swing low, chariot, swing low, low, etc.

4—Prayer, prayer is de way, way, etc.

5—Let God's people git 'board,'board, etc.

6—Gwine to heaven on de mor-en-ing
train, train, etc.

7—My Lord send a me here, here,
My Lord send a me here, to pray.

8—Do thyself a no harm, harm.

Railroad songs are so named from the fact that they are sung by large bodies of men in the construction of railroads and other public works. Not many of them originated on the railroad, but their use in the army building fortifications, and in these more modern kinds of labor, has probably served to elongate them. The wise contractor employing colored men at work of this character lets them sing. The songs require little expenditure of breath, and are long drawn, monotonous chants. They usually have a Scripture theme, and often tell at length a long Scripture story with the negro's own improvements and interpretations thrown in. The refrain comes at considerable and irregular intervals, just often enough to quicken the lagging interest of any who may have dropped out. Only the leader attempts to sing the words, though perhaps a few nearest him catch a strain here and there; but the tune, which often runs along for a dozen verses between *la* and *do*, is hummed by others far and near, and gives the time to which the spades sink into the clay or the picks descend.

To hear these songs, not all of which are religious, at their best, one needs to hear them in a rock tunnel. The men are hurried in after an explosion to drill with speed for another double row of blasts. They work two and two, one holding and turning the drill, the other striking it with a sledge. The sledges descend in unison as the long low chant gives the time. I wonder if the reader can

imagine the effect of it all, the powder smoke filling the place, the darkness made barely visible by the little lights on the hats of the men, the echoing sounds of men and mules toward the outlet loading and carting away the rock thrown out by the last blast, and the men at the heading droning their low chant to the *chink! chink!* of the steel. A single musical phrase or a succession of a half dozen notes caught on a visit to such a place sticks in one's mind forever. Even as I write I seem to be in a tunnel of this description and to hear the sharp metallic stroke and the syncopated chant.

One occasionally hears these long songs in an evening meeting. They are interminable, and the only way to end them is to stop. One of them, a part of which has been published, and the whole of which no one man knows, is "Walk Jerusalem just like John." Different versions of it have been printed, but none like the one I have.

This song throws in almost at random couplets like:

Walk around from do' to do',
What to do I did not know;

Walk Jerusalem on Zion's hill,
Walk about on heaven and earth;

Satan thought he had me fast,
Thank the Lord I'm free at last.

I bless the Lord I'm going to die,
I'm going to judgment by and by.

Oh, John he heard the trumpet blow,
Hills and mountains fall below.

It has no proper end. It goes on at the will of the leader, and, unlike the ordinary hymn, which may be ended either with a stanza or the refrain and usually is meant to end with the latter, this is meant never to end so far as the structure of the song is concerned. It may end with "When

I come to die," or "Jes' like John"; but in either case it gives the air of incompleteness, like the old Scotch and Irish songs which ended so often on *re* and were ready to begin again. Some of these songs have a proper end, and may stop with the refrain any time; but the refrain is of variable occurrence, and may come every two lines, or run on for an epitomized biography of some Bible character.

WALK JERUSALEM JES' LIKE JOHN.

While the narrative portions of this song and others like it are used as a solo, which is a great saving of breath, there is a humming accompaniment, with many an "Amen" and "Yes," and frequently a chuckle or "holy laugh," especially at any suggestion of giving the devil what is conceived to be his due, or of any sharp turn of Providence for the worsting of sinners. One of these songs, which I have heard both on the railroad and

in an evening meeting, is "The New Burying Ground."

NEW BURYING GROUND.

2—All along down by de watery shore,
De waters run steady, level as a die;
Hearse come down next day gone by;
Take de lill babe to new burying
  ground.
Yes, I went down to the valley to pray,
Met ole Satan on de way.
Look out, Satan, out my way!
Took my sword an' cut him down;
Satan shot one ball at me:
Missed my soul and got my sin.

Refrain.

3—O, no, brethering, dat ain't all,—
Golden girdle round my waist,
Starry crown upon my head,
Palm of victory in my hand.

Refrain.

4—I went to meeting on a certain day,
Went fo' to hear what de preacher say.
Bout de time dat I got in,
Spoke one word condemned my sin.
Went back home an' counted de cost,
Heard what a treasure I had lost.

Refrain.

5—Yes, mysteree! Come and see!
Heard a great voice shoutin' in de new
  buryin' ground.
B for book and be forgiven,
Wrote by wise men sent from heaven.
If you want to go to heaven when you
  dies,
Stop you long tongue from telling lies.
Stars a-fallin'! God's a-callin'!
Don't dat look like judgment day?

Refrain.

6—I went down by the tottery sho'.
Found a ship all ready to go.
Cap'n he come, troubled in mind,
"Wake up! wake up, you sleep, sleepy
  man!"
O, cap'n, if it's me,
Pray you cast me overboard!
Cast Brer Jonah overboard;
Whale did swaller Brer Jonah whole.
Three long nights, three long days,
Jonah lied in de body of de whale.
Las' words I hear Brer Jonah say,
He had no place to lie his head.
God commanded fish to land,
Cast Brer Jonah on dry sand.
Gourd vine growed all over his head.
Inchworm come long and cut it down.

Refrain.

7—Hit 'em wid de hammer cryin', "Sin-
  ner, repent!"
Wrought sorrow in de Jedge-e-ment.
Green trees burn, and why not dry?
Sinner man die, and why not I?
Sea ob glass all full of fire.
I'm gwine to jine God's heavenly choir.

H for Hannah, happy was she,
Lill boy Samuel on her knee.
B for book an' God forgiven,
Young child Jesus came from heaven.

Refrain.

8—Sing ole hymn at new buryin' ground,
Dar gwine lay his body down.
He gave me pree, and sot me free
An' bought my soul from libertee.
Death come along at break of day,
Take de lill baby on his way.
Give me a horn and tell me to blow,
Come along, don't you want to go?
Bell done ring, angels done sing,
God A'mighty bought my heart and
  tongue.
Went down hill, fell on my knees,
Help me, Jesus, if you please.

Refrain.

Another of these is "How Long
Watch-a-Man?" The melody of this
is worthy of special attention. It is
sweet, full, dignified and descriptive.
The variations of "Watch-a-man" are
very telling, and the repeated and re-
tarded final tonic notes, suggestive of
the passing of time as seen by the
"Watch-a-man" are fine. It deserves
to be fitted with a strong, full harmony and to be widely known. I consider it a gem. It is partly in 3:4 and
partly in 4:4 time, and the fitting of
these into a smooth, flowing melody
in perfect taste is noteworthy. The
words are not so good.

HOW LONG, WATCHMAN?

O how long, watch-a-man? How long,

watch-a-man, How long, watch-a-man?

FINE.

How long, watch-a-man? How long?

1. { How long did it rain? Can any one tell? }
   { For for-ty days and nights it fell. }

D C.

How long, watch-a-man? How long?

2—Oh, dey called ole Noah foolish man,
Built his ark upon dry sand.
Foolish Jews come a-ridin' by,
Hawk and spit on Noah's timber.
My sister done broke de ice an' gone
Sitting in heaven wid 'er raiment on.

Refrain.

3—Watah come up to de cellah door,
Marched an' slipped on de upper floor,
Den I went up to de winder an' peep
out;
I see ole Noah passin' by,
Try an' help me out er my miseree.
I know ole Noah felt and seen,
I b'lieve God A'mighty locked de door.
Come along my muddah to de watah
side,
Come along an' be baptized.

Refrain.

4—My dungeon open, my chains flew wide,
Glory to God, I've found him at last.
Brer Jonah lied in de bowels ub de
whale,
Brer Jonah prayed in de bowels ub de
whale.
De ark got stuck on de mountain-top,
God commanded de rain to stop.
De rainbow show, de sun he shine,
Glory to God, my sins are forgiven.

Refrain.

5—How long was Noah buildin' of de ark?
Mo'n a hundred years he kept to work.

6—How long was Jonah in the bowels of
the whale?
For three whole days and nights he
sailed.

7—How long will the righteous in heaven
be?
For ever and ever their Lord they see.

A good many people, no one of
whom knew it all, contributed first
and last to give the foregoing hymn
the degree of completeness which is
here shown.
The negro is reluctant to bring a
service to a close. When, late at
night, the end finally comes, there is
often a quotation concerning the
heavenly assembly:

"Where congregations ne'er break up,
And Sabbaths have no end."

The thought enters several of their
own songs, among them one of the
interminable ones such as we are now

considering. It runs on in narrative
form with long or short stanzas, but
calls for active and repeated responses
in the refrain, "I believe!" The refrain changes, also, from time to time,
to suit the tenor of the stanzas, but
the end is always the same, "And
Sabbath has no end."

SABBATH HAS NO END.

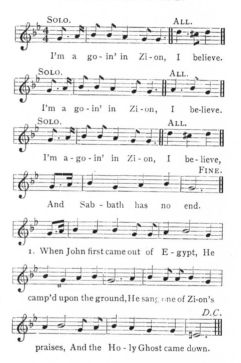

2—He done blessed him and cheered him
And told him not to weep,
For the power was in Christ Jesus
To raise him from his sleep.

Refrain.

Mighty meeting in Zion,
I believe,
Mighty meeting in Zion,
I believe,
Mighty meeting in Zion,
I believe,
And Sabbath has no end.

3—When Jesus came to the world,
He came to do no harm,
But they placed on him a thorny crown,
And the blood came streaming down.

Refrain.

Wasn't that a shame?
  I believe,
Wasn't that a shame?
  I believe,
Wasn't that a shame?
  I believe,
And Sabbath has no end.

4—Not all the blood of beasts
  On Jewish altars slain
Could give a guilty conscience peace,
  Or wash away the stain.
Behold he wore the mortgage,
  He was Almighty God;
At once they might have 'stroyed him,
  But he saved them by his word.

Refrain.

I know, 'twas Jesus,
  I believe,
I know, 'twas Jesus,
  I believe,
I know, 'twas Jesus,
  I believe,
And Sabbath has no end.

5—Want you to look at you dying Saviour,
  Want you to look at you dying Lord;
Stand near the cross and view him,
  Behold the Lamb of God.
They rebuked him and they scorned him,
  And told him to come down,
Before the cross of suffering,
  They changed him for his crown.
Jesus came in many mysterious ways,
  His wonders to perform,
He placed his footsteps in the seas,
  And rode upon the storm.

Refrain.

I'm going to heaven,
  I believe,
I'm going to heaven,
  I believe,
I'm going to heaven,
  I believe,
 And Sabbath has no end.

6—They took my blessed Jesus,
  And led him to the whiteoak island,
They hewed him out a yoke,
  And they yoked it on to him.
His ankle bones they done give way,
  His knees they smote the ground,
And every star shall disappear,
  King Jesus shall be mine.

Refrain.

I'm going to Zion,
  I believe,
I'm going to Zion,
  I believe,
I'm going to Zion,
  I believe,
And Sabbath has no end.

7—I met old Judas at the spring.
  The history how he talked,—
"For thirty pieces of silver,
  I show you where my Jesus walk."

Refrain.

Walked the road to heaven,
  I believe,
Walked the road to heaven,
  I believe,
Walked the road to heaven,
  I believe,
And Sabbath has no end.

8—Mary saw her father coming,
  Done run and met him too,
She told him 'bout her brother,
  Who was dead and passed away.

Refrain.

Then come forth Lazarus,
  I believe,
Then come forth Lazarus,
  I believe,
Then come forth Lazarus,
  I believe,
And Sabbath has no end.

9—Well, they taken my blessed Jesus,
  They led him to the low ground of sorrow,
They hewed him out a Roman cross,
  They placed it on his shoulder.
They speared him long in his side!
They speared him long in his side!
  (Wasn't that a shame!)
There came out water and blood!
There came out water and blood!
  (O my Lord!)
The blood was for redemption,
  The water for baptism.

Refrain.

So we'll rock trouble over,
  I believe,
So we'll rock trouble over,
  I believe,
So we'll rock trouble over,
  I believe,
And Sabbath has no end.

This last hymn I have heard in different places, but the part relating to the crucifixion I have not heard except at religious services. The last of these hymns which I shall give is one that I heard but once. I do not know that it is used as a song to work with, but suspect that the "ham-mer-ring!" which is the constant response, may be used sometimes to time the descent of the pick or sledge. As I heard it, however, it was sung at an evening meeting, a single voice telling the story, repeating twice each line, while the congregation sang a heavy bass "Ham-mer-ring!"

THE CHRISTIANS' HYMN OF THE CRUCIFIXION.

2—Mary wept (Ham-mer-ring)
And Martha mourned. (Ham-mer-ring)
If thou'd been here, (Ham-mer-ring)
My brother hadn't died. (Ham-mer-ring)
They buried him, (Ham-mer-ring)
And on the third day (Ham-mer-ring)
He ascended high, (Ham-mer-ring)
To his Father's house. (Ham-mer-ring)
Jesus came, (Ham-mer-ring)
His friend he rise, (Ham-mer-ring)
And found a home (Ham-mer-ring)
Above the skies. (Ham-mer-ring)
O. Lazarus, (Ham-mer-ring)
I know Lazarus! (Ham-mer-ring)
Come forth, Lazarus! (Ham-mer-ring)
Want you to loose him (Ham-mer-ring)
And let him go. (Ham-mer-ring.)

A good many of these railroad songs, I am satisfied, originated in those grewsome vigils wherein a dozen or more people "sit up" with the dead. The night is largely spent in singing, and the set songs run out long before morning. The family sleep, or are supposed to sleep, often in the same room, and if not there then in a room within easy hearing distance, and the singing is thought to comfort them, as well as to help in keeping the watchers awake and to apply the occasion to the profit of those present. The song about "The New Burying Ground" is evidently of this kind. Its references to the little babe that had been taken, the mother left behind, and to the next day as that of the burial, plainly show its original meaning; but it is sung now on other and very different occasions.

These songs are long, low, monotonous croons, wherein the recitative is half sung, half spoken, and the voices other than that of the leader merely hum with occasional ejaculations and an intermittent refrain. The songs are modified by their subsequent uses, but originating, as they do, without a distinct purpose to make a song, they are most irregular in everything but rhythm, which is always such that they can be swayed to and patted with the foot. They afford a good illustration of the way in which the more elaborate songs originate.

There are some of the more recent plantation hymns which have added an element of culture without diminishing religious fervor. One of the best of these is "Were You There When They Crucified My Lord?" It dwells on the details of the crucifixion, and the separate stanzas add only a single line each to the song. It is a tender and beautiful hymn, the climax of its effect depending largely on the hold and slur on the exclamation "Oh!" with which the third line begins, and the repetition and expression of the word *"tremble! tremble! tremble!"*

WERE YOU THERE?

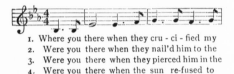

1. Where you there when they cru - ci - fied my
2. Were you there when they nail'd him to the
3. Were you there when they pierced him in the
4. Were you there when the sun re-fused to

Lord?   (Were   you there?) Were   you
cross?   (Were   you there?) Were   you
side?   (Were   you there?) Were   you
shine?   (Were   you there?) Were   you
ad lib.

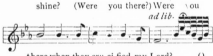

there when they cru-ci-fied my Lord?   O
there when they nail'd him to the cross?   O
there when they pierced him in the side?   O
there when the sun refused to shine?   O

some-times   it caus - es   me   to
some-times   it caus - es   me   to
some-times   it caus - es   me   to
some-times   it caus - es   me   to

rit.   *p*   *pp*

trem - ble! trem-ble! trem - ble! Were you
trem - ble! trem-ble! trem - ble! Were you
trem - ble! trem-ble! trem - ble! Were you
trem - ble! trem-ble! trem - ble! Were you

there when they cru - ci - fied my Lord?
there when they nail'd him to the cross?
there when they pierced him in the side?
there when the sun re - fused to shine?

PETER ON THE SEA.

1. Pe - ter! (Pe - ter,) Pe - ter, (Pe - ter,)
2. Ga - briel! (Ga-briel,) Ga-briel, (Ga-briel,)
3. Who did(who did) Jo - nah?(who did?)
4. Whale did(whale did) Jo - nah!(whale did!)
5. Dan - iel(Dan - iel) li - on's (Dan - iel!)

Pe - ter   on   the sea, sea, sea, sea!
Ga-briel,blow your trump,trump,trump,trump!
Who   did swal - low Jo - nah, Jo - nah?
Whale did swal - low Jo - nah, Jo - nah?
Dan - iel   in   the li - on's, . li - on's!

Pe - ter, (Pe - ter,) Pe - ter, (Pe - ter,)
Ga - briel, (Ga - briel,)Ga - briel, (Ga -briel,)
Who   did (who did)   Jo - nah? (who did?)
Whale did(whale did)   Jo - nah!(whale did!)
Dan - iel (Dan - iel)   li - on's (Dan - iel!)

Pe - ter   on   the sea, sea, sea, sea!
Ga - briel,blow your trump,trump,trump,trump!
Who   did swal - low Jo - nah, Jo - nah?
Whale did swal - low Jo - nah, Jo - nah!
Dan - iel   in   the li - on's, li - on's!

Pe - ter, (Pe - ter,) Pe - ter, (Pet - er,)
Ga - briel, (Ga - briel,) Ga - briel, (Gabri-el,)
Who   did (who did) Jo - nah? (who did?)
Whale did (whale did) Jo - nah! (whale did!)
Dan - iel (Dan - iel)   li - on's, (Dan - iel!)

Pe - ter   on   the sea, sea, sea, sea!
Ga-briel,blow your,trump,trump,trump,trump!
ho   did swal - low Jo - nah, Jo - nah?
hale did swal - low Jo - nah, Jo - nah!
Dan - iel   in   the li - on's, li - on's!

Pe - ter   on   the   sea,   sea!
Ga - briel,   blow   your   trump - et!
Who   did   swal - low   Jo - nah?
Whale   did   swal - low   Jo - nah!
Dan - iel   in   the   li - on's!

Pe - ter   on the sea,   sea,   sea!
Ga - briel, blow your trump - et,   blow!
Who did swal - low Jo - nah?   Who?
Whale did swal - low Jo - nah!   Whale!
Dan - iel   in   the li - on's den!

The foregoing modern song keeps much of the spirit of the older ones. It is in striking contrast with the preceding song. It is a lively staccato, is full of responses, is not in the least shy of the fourth and seventh notes, and is thoroughly up to date except perhaps in its theology. No higher criticism has yet eliminated from negro theology a vestige of the miraculous. Peter on the sea, Gabriel with his trumpet, Jonah and the whale and Daniel in the lions' den are all here in a swift-moving panorama, and with a lively good humor that is nothing less than mirth-provoking.

One of the most interesting places in which I have ever attended worship is a well built and fairly well appointed meeting house erected by the colored people, well out in the country, and adorned with crude frescoes that show a desire to beautify the sanctuary of the Lord. I have been there in summer when the temperature of the day did not exceed that of the meeting, and I have been there in winter when the minister announced that he was "cold, brethren; cold two ways, cold in de body and cold speritually"; and yet I have never been wholly disappointed in seeing something worth while. The records of the business meeting of Saturday are read on Sunday morning with a good many exclusions from the church "for immoral conduct," as the charge has invariably read when I have been there; and not infrequently there are people to be received into membership with ecstatic experiences proved by a repetition of them on the spot. The preaching begins very moderately, but as one after another comes to the front, the tide rises until the preacher in charge, who is said to have been the longest settled pastor in Kentucky, rises and begins; and then there is a demonstration. The company has long been swaying back and forth in the rhythm of the preacher's chant, and now and then there has come a shout of assent to the oft repeated text. Each time the preacher's almost incoherent talk

becomes articulate in a shout, "I have trod de wine-press," there are cries of "Yes!" "Praise de Lawd!" and "Glory!" from the Amen corner, where sit the "praying brethren," and the Hallelujah corner, where sit the "agonizing sistering." In the earlier demonstrations the men rather lead, but from the time when Aunt Melinda cries out "Nebbah mind de wite folks! My soul's happy! Hallelujah!" and leaps into the air, the men are left behind. Women go off into trances, roll under benches, or go spinning down the aisle with eyes closed and with arms outstretched. Each shout of the preacher is the signal for some one else to start; and, strange to say, though there are two posts in the aisle, and the women go spinning down like tops, I never saw one strike a post. I have seen the pastor on a day when the house would not contain the multitude cause the seats to be turned and take his own position in the door with a third of the audience inside and the rest without, and have heard him provoke the most ecstatic response to a reference to his wife such as this, "O, I love dat yaller woman out dar in dat buggy, but I love my Jesus bettah!" I have seen the minister in grave danger of being dragged out of the pulpit by some of the shouters who in their ecstasy laid hold upon him. I have seen an old man stand in the aisle and jump eighty-nine times after I began to count, and without moving a muscle of his thin, parchment-like face, and without disturbing the meeting.

There is more or less variation in the service at this church, but there is one invariable feature, the collection; and the more white people there are present, the more important is this feature. Two deacons sit at a table in front of the pulpit; a song is sung, and the contributors walk up the aisle and deposit their contributions amid exhortations and plaudits thrown in at the end of the line. Each coin is scrutinized, and there is no opportunity to pass a mutilated coin at par, as some people do in dealing with the Lord, or make a button do duty for legal tender. One day some one started a new fashioned hymn, and the people came up slowly. The preacher interrupted the hymn midway saying, "Breddern, dah hain't no money in dat tune. Sing one of de good ole tunes." In response to this suggestion they sang "Jes' gwine ober in de heabenlye lan'." It has a high air, covering only a diminished fifth, and running mostly on the tonic note, but the monotony is broken and a decided character is given to the melody in the refrain, "De heabenlye lan'," when from the last syllable of "heabenlye" to "lan'" the voice rises from E flat tonic to D flat, which it holds with a strong accent on a half note filling the last half of the measure.

JES' GWINE OBER IN DE HEABENLYE LAN'.

I { You can hinder me here,but you can't do it there,
For He sits in de heavens,and He answers prayer,

Jes' gwine o - ber in de heabenlye lan'!

REFRAIN.

De heabenlye lan', Heab-en-lye lan',

Jes' gwine o - ber in de heabenlye lan'!

2—Sinnah jine de church an' he run pretty well,
Jes' gwine ober in de heabenlye lan'!
An' afore six weeks he's on his road to hell,
Jes' gwine ober in de heabenlye lan'!
De heabenlye lan'!
De heabenlye lan'!
Jes' gwine ober in de heabenlye lan'!

3—Hebben is a high an' a lofty place,
Jes' gwine ober in de heabenlye lan'!
But yer can't git dah ef you hain't got de grace,
Jes' gwine ober in de heabenlye lan'!
De heabenlve lan'!
De heabenlye lan'!
Jes' gwine ober in de heabenlye lan'!

4—Satan he's like a snake in de grass,
Jes' gwine ober in de heabenlye lan'!

An' ef you don' mind he'll git you at las',
Jes' gwine ober in de heabenlye lan'!
De heabenlye lan'!
De heabenlye lan'!
Jes' gwine ober in de heabenlye lan'!

5—Way ober yander in de harves' fiel',
Jes' gwine ober in de heabenlye lan'!
De angels are rollin' at de chariot wheel,
Jes' gwine ober in de heabenlye lan'!
De heabenlye lan'!
De heabenlye lan'!
Jes' gwine ober in de heabenlye lan'!

What conception the worshipers have of an angel is patent, for two of them are wrought into the frescoes of the room. The feet of one turn abruptly to the right, and the feet of the other to the left. One of them is cross eyed; both are white. There was every indication that this song brought a good collection.

A good many of the negro songs are written in the pentatonic scale. The same is true of a majority of Scotch songs and the songs of Oriental nations. When Luther W. Mason went to Japan to teach our system of music in the government schools, he sought out melodies common among us that are written in the scale of five notes. The first which he taught and which they received with great pleasure was one that we received from the Orient, I think from India, "There is a happy land." Few of the thousands of thousands who have sung this air all round the world have thought how a part of its hold upon so many million of hearts is its omission of the two notes 4 and 7 from the diatonic scale. Several of the best of the Scotch songs are of this character, as "Auld Lang Syne," and, with the exception of one or two notes which I believe are modern, "Annie Laurie." It is a little strange that just when the breaking up of Primrose and West's minstrel troupe might seem to indicate, and probably does indicate, a decline of interest in the burnt cork show that has been so popular for generations, and still is popular in England, there should be a great increase of so called "coon songs," some of whose airs are very pleasing, arranged for the piano. To any one who desires to write a fair imitation of a characteristic negro melody, one simple rule is good to start with: compose it on the black keys of the piano. It takes more than this rule, however, to make a good negro song, and the best of them are ill adapted to a piano. The violin or banjo fits them best, for they have no frets to distribute the error in tone. A sharp and B flat are not mathematically the same, but they must be represented by one tone on the piano. The negro is able to make this fine discrimination when he uses accidentals, and this makes it impossible to represent the tones exactly upon the staff; but the five notes of the simpler scale suffice for most of the hymns. "In Dat Great Day" is an example of a song whose tune is major and which ranges over an octave and a half with no suggestion of a lack of sufficient tone variety. There is great contrast between the startling warning, almost breathless, "Whah you runnin', sinnah?" and the clear, exultant "O Is-a-rel" The entire piece is of great power. It is a negro *Dies Iræ*. The use of the major is all the more remarkable because the eschatological theme and the sombre succession of incidents described would naturally suggest the minor.

This song illustrates a way in which the negro varies his melodies. In theory the song is sung in unison, and there is no harmony proper. But in practice the more independent singers introduce grace notes and slurs, and the higher and lower voices range above and below in fifths and thirds in the more descriptive portions, especially in the latter verses. In this song the melody of "O Isarel! O Isarel!" is given in the first line where those words are used, and in the notes which run nearest the tonic; but as the song proceeds this simple theme is worked out quite elaborately and with much greater variety than the notes here given indicate, but in a manner which they illustrate.

IN THAT GREAT DAY.

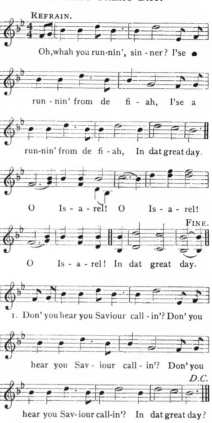

2—Don' you see de dead arisin'? etc.

3—Don' you heah de trumpet soundin'?

4—Don' you see dem tombs a-bustin'?

5—Yes, we'll see our chillen risin'.

6—Don' you see de chariot comin'?

7—Don' you see de sinnah tremblin'?

8—Don' you heah de saints a-shoutin'?

This quaint *Dies Iræ* may well be paired with an equally quaint "Hallelujah Churus." It is a Baptist hymn, "Been down into the Sea." Its exultant hallelujahs suggest, as one hears them, some passages in Handel's great masterpiece. I cannot expect any one to agree with this statement who merely picks out the notes on the piano; but one who hears the piece sung by a great congregation will not think the statement wholly extravagant.

BEEN DOWN INTO THE SEA.

4—Hallelujah! an' a hallelujah!
Hallelujah, Lord! I've been down into the sea!
Yes, I've been to the sea and I've been babtized,
  Been down into the sea;
I've been babtized in Jesus' name,
  Been down into the sea!
Hallelujah! an' a hallelujah!
Hallelujah, Lord! I've been down into the sea!

Now and then there is a piece that not only uses the diatonic scale, but makes the most of it. One effective song, "When the Chariot Comes," uses the seven toned scale, and emphasizes the fact by the prominence of its major thirds. For instance, the first time the word "comes" is used, it is cut into five syllables with emphatic rough breathings, and fitted to a *do-sol-mi-sol-do.*

WHEN THE CHARIOT COMES.

2—King Jesus, he'll be driver, when she cu-hu-hu-hu-hums, etc.

3—She'll be loaded with bright angels, etc.

4—She will neither rock nor totter, etc.

5—She will run so level and steady, etc.

6—She will take us to the portills, etc.

2—Hallelujah! an' a hallelujah!
Hallelujah, Lord! I've been down into the sea!
Why don' dem mourners rise an' tell—
  Been down into the sea—
The glories of Immanuel?
  Been down into the sea!

3—Hallelujah! an' a hallelujah!
Hallelujah, Lord! I've been down into the sea!
I do believe without a doubt—
  Been down into the sea—
That a Christian has a right to shout,
  Been down into the sea!

Among the eschatological songs, I do not remember any that have affected me as did the song, "Who's Dat Yandah?" At the end of each inquiry, "Who's dat yandah?" is a rest of two beats in the middle of the measure; and the effect is more startling than the syncopation of a note. It is an emphasized silence of eager and fearful expectancy. It is a pure minor, and runs almost wholly in thirds. This song is so painfully realistic in its tone picturing as to cause an involuntary turning of the head in expectation of some majestic Presence. It starts with a refrain, which is repeated after every stanza and again at the end, as is usually the case where the song opens with the refrain.

2—Sinnah, sinnah, you'd bettah pray,
    Looks like-a my Lord comin' in de sky!
Or you' soul be los' at de jedgment day,
    Looks like-a my Lord comin' in de sky!

3—Wait till I gits in de middle of de air,
    Won't be nary sinnah dere.

4—De debbil is a liar and a conjurer, too,
    An' ef you don' mind he'll conjure you.

5—I nebbah can fo'git de day,
    When Jesus washed my sins away.

6—Washed my haid in de midnight dew,
    De mawning star's a witness, too.

7—Sinnahs jines de church, and dey sing and dey shout,
    An' afore six months des all turned out.

8—When I was a mourner jes' like you,
    My knees got 'quainted wid de hillside, too.

WHO'S DAT YANDAH?

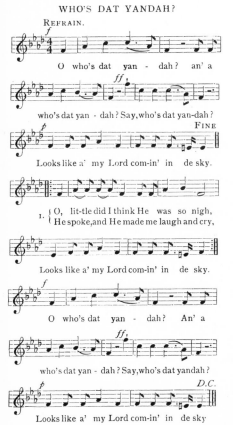

In this and the two preceding articles I have given nearly seventy of these songs. It has been a sincere pleasure to prepare them for preservation in this form. Growing out of the heart experience of the negro, the older ones are absolutely natural and unaffected, and exhibit no attempt to express the religious life in conventional terms. Even their crudest oddities are of interest as data for study in religious and social development, and this is by no means the limit of their value.

I have not counted it a part of my duty to write harmonies for these songs, but have endeavored to preserve the melodies as accurately as possible.

These songs are such excellent exponents of "heart religion" that they are certain to disappear before the swift coming "book religion," save as they are carefully recorded and preserved. I exhort all teachers, pastors and others who are able to secure these songs to do so, with the music wherever possible, and to see that they are suitably preserved in print.